Gallantry in action: Second Lieutenant Leach leads men of the Royal Lancaster Regiment against German trenches at Wieltje, Ypres, in May 1915. Although wounded, he pressed home the attack and captured a German standard. For his gallantry he was awarded the newly established Military Cross.

British Gallantry Awards
1855–2000

Peter Duckers

Published in 2011 by Shire Publications Ltd,
Midland House, West Way, Botley, Oxford OX2 0PH, UK.
Website: www.shirebooks.co.uk

Copyright © 2001 by Peter Duckers.
First published 2001. Reprinted 2005, 2010 and 2011.
Shire Library 394. ISBN 978 0 74780 516 8.

Peter Duckers is hereby identified as the author of this
work in accordance with Section 77 of the Copyright,
Designs and Patents Act, 1988.

British Library Cataloguing in Publication Data:
Duckers, Peter
British gallantry awards 1855–2000.
– (Shire Library; no. 394)
1. Military decorations – Great Britain – History
I. Title 355.1'342'0941
ISBN 978 0 74780 516 8

COVER: The Distinguished Service Medal (DSM) with
associated medals for 1914-18 service: the 1914-15 Star
and British War Medal.

ACKNOWLEDGEMENT
The author would like to thank the Trustees of the
Shropshire Regimental Museum in Shrewsbury Castle for
permission to use some of the original photographs and
medals in the museum collection.

Printed in China through Worldprint Ltd.

Contents

The first Indian Victoria Cross. At Zillebeke on 31st October 1914 Sepoy (Private) Khudadad Khan, 129th Baluchis, keeps his machine gun in action under heavy fire, with all his comrades dead around him. Severely wounded himself, he was left for dead when the Germans overran the trench and later crawled away. He was the first Indian to receive the VC after the award was opened to them in 1911. All the other members of the gun team were posthumously awarded the Indian Order of Merit or the Indian Distinguished Service Medal.

Early unofficial and regimental awards

Bravery in battle has been recognised through the ages. The way that it has been rewarded has varied over time, but it seems to have been the Greeks who first gave wearable badges as distinctions. The idea was taken up by the Romans, who established a regular system of military rewards including bronze or silver badges that soldiers could wear on their armour as a visible indication that they had been honoured for gallantry. Such rewards are sometimes depicted on the gravestones of Roman soldiers.

In Britain, the granting of medals to recognise gallantry in battle can be traced to the Civil Wars of 1642–51. A number of different military rewards were established, for example the Earl of Manchester's Medal and Sir Thomas Fairfax's Medal of 1645. Some were simply tokens of regard or awards for faithful service, but others constitute the first medals awarded for acts of gallantry. Robert Welch and John Smith were each given a gold medal for bravery at Edgehill in 1642, when they recovered the King's colours. It is known that these men, and others rewarded in similar ways, wore their medals stitched on to the sashes of their uniform – perhaps the origin of wearing medals suspended from pieces of ribbon.

The germ of a standardised system of official gallantry awards seems to appear in the mid seventeenth century; the Commonwealth Naval Medals of 1649–50 and 1658 (for the campaign of 1653) were

Above: A 'military reward' badge of the English Civil War, c.1644–5. Little is known about the recipients or circumstances of these early medals but some were clearly granted for gallantry in action.

One of the Commonwealth Naval Medals, awarded in 1658 for service against the Dutch in 1653 during Britain's brief republican period. The type shown here was granted to captains who distinguished themselves in action. The design features the shields of England, Scotland and Ireland over an anchor.

The Naval Reward of 1665. Obverse with King Charles II in Roman costume. Like the Commonwealth Naval Medals, these medals were given for service against the Dutch.

specifically to reward individuals for bravery in naval actions. Although these became obsolete at the Restoration in 1660, official Naval Rewards were re-established for the Dutch Wars by Charles II in 1665 and continued under William and Mary. However, despite these promising beginnings the system did not develop and in the eighteenth century there was a return to *ad hoc* rewards, produced only as and when required.

In the later eighteenth century it became common for regimental officers, individuals and even societies to award medals. Not surprisingly, greater interest was aroused during major wars, when the activities of the nation's armed forces were widely reported and acts of gallantry brought to notice. During the French Wars of 1793–1815 a system of unofficial gallantry medals and badges emerged. Many of these awards were sponsored (and paid for) by the commanding officer or other officers of a particular regiment and the evidence suggests that they were worn in uniform and were greatly prized. The production of unofficial awards continued long

A regimental medal for the Peninsular War. An example of the many different unofficial types produced by British regiments during the French Wars of 1793–1815, this one was awarded to Major A. M'Intosh, 85th Light Infantry, for gallantry at the Battle of Fuentes d'Onoro in Spain in 1811.

The Army Gold Medal, 'small type' as awarded to field officers. These were conferred very sparingly (596 in total) during the French Wars. Although in essence for distinguished service, some were awarded for gallantry under fire. The medal is encased in a glazed frame, the name of the battle being engraved on the reverse, within a wreath.

Below: *The regimental award of the 2nd–53rd (Shropshire) Regiment, granted to sergeants for bravery in the Peninsular War, 1809–14. This example was given to Sergeant Thomas Cox (named on the reverse) for his gallantry at Salamanca in 1812.*

after the end of the French Wars, a famous example being Sir Harry Smith's Medal for Gallantry issued in 1851 to about thirty soldiers of the Cape Mounted Rifles for bravery in action in South Africa. Unofficial awards were also made to native Indian forces, some being known for the Afghan War of 1839–42.

There are grounds for considering the official Army Gold Medals, Naval Gold Medals and Army Gold Crosses awarded only to officers between 1793 and 1815 as a form of gallantry medal since some were given for leadership 'under fire'. However, they are usually regarded as distinguished service awards. Similarly, although many of the unofficial medals of 1793–1815 were for meritorious service or simply for presence in a number of actions (there being no official campaign medals at the time), some *were* undoubtedly for gallantry. For example, the 2nd–53rd (Shropshire) Regiment instituted a reward in 1815 for sergeants who had distinguished themselves in action in the Peninsular War. The medals were issued by the commanding officer, Sir Thomas Bingham, on the instructions of the Colonel of the Regiment, Sir John

Badge of a Companion of the Order of the Bath. This level of the Order, which dates back to 1725, was created in 1815 to reward junior officers but later came to be regarded as a distinguished service award often given to officers for long and meritorious service. Some, however, were conferred for specific acts of gallantry.

Abercromby. Only fifteen sergeants received the award, 'to be worn on the left breast'. Similar decorations were instituted by many regiments but as they were issued only in small numbers they are now rare; they are fully detailed in J. L. Balmer's *Regimental and Volunteer Medals* (Langlands, 1988).

At the end of the Waterloo campaign in 1815 the Order of the Bath was extended to include a new military division, in which the Companionship of the Order (CB) was specifically intended to enable rewards to be given to junior officers who had rendered distinguished service. As before, the CB came to be recognised more as a reward for distinguished service, sometimes over a long period, rather than as a decoration for bravery in a particular action. Despite this, it continued to be the only decoration available to officers for such services until the establishment of the Victoria Cross in 1856 and the Distinguished Service Order in 1886, and some were undoubtedly granted to reward gallantry on campaign.

The Honourable East India Company can be regarded as the real originator of a standardised system of decorations. In 1837 it inaugurated the Indian Order of Merit for its Indian soldiers. Its three classes were, until the institution of the Indian Distinguished Service Medal in 1907, the only gallantry awards available to native Indian

7

Above left: *The Indian Order of Merit. Instituted in 1837 for the Honourable East India Company's Indian soldiers and regarded as the first official award for gallantry in action. Shown here is the Third Class, along with the medal for the Afghan War of 1878–80, awarded to a soldier of the 21st Punjabis for gallantry in the Shutagardan Pass in 1879.*

Above right: *A group containing the Indian Order of Merit. This Third Class was awarded for gallantry in defence of Fort Cavagnari on the Samana ridge in 1897. It also shows the India General Service Medal (1895–1902) with four clasps and the 1911 Delhi Durbar Medal, for the Coronation of George V as Emperor of India.*

troops. The medals were awarded solely for bravery in action, carried a financial reward and were very highly regarded. Recipients technically had to be in possession of one class before they could be advanced to a higher grade. The Order was taken over by the Crown in 1858 following the Indian Mutiny and continued to be awarded until 1947, when India became independent.

Winning the Indian Order of Merit: Lance Naik (Lance Corporal) Guzain was awarded the Indian Order of Merit, Second Class, for his gallantry in attacking German trenches on 23rd November 1914. To get a better shot at the enemy, he lay out in the open at different points, disregarding enemy fire and the great danger to himself.

8

British troops in the Crimea. As well as large, set-piece battles such as Alma, Inkermann and Balaklava, it was the day-to-day fighting in the trenches 'before Sebastopol' which led to demands for the creation of specific awards for gallantry. The Distinguished Conduct Medal, Conspicuous Gallantry Medal and Victoria Cross were the result.

Official awards and the Crimean War, 1854–6

The British government was only finally spurred into establishing a regular system of gallantry awards by the conditions of a major European conflict: the Crimean War of 1854–6.

In 1854 Britain, the Ottoman Empire, France and Sardinia went to war against Russia – Britain's first European war since 1815. Although remembered as the 'Crimean War' because Britain and France campaigned on the Crimean peninsula in the Black Sea, the war was actually fought at any potential point of contact with Russia – the Baltic, the White Sea, the Black Sea, the Sea of Azoff, around the Danube, and even in the Far East on Russia's Pacific coast. However, it was the nature of the fighting on land endured by British forces in the Crimea, coupled with their terrible suffering through bad administration, cold and disease, which captured contemporary interest. The fighting was widely reported by the first real war correspondents, principal amongst whom was William Howard Russell of *The Times*, and news of the war's progress was eagerly followed. Incidents like 'the Charge of the Light Brigade' at Balaklava in October 1854 fired the popular imagination. The war, centred on the siege of the Russian naval base at Sebastopol, dragged on far longer than expected. It was the almost daily acts of bravery by soldiers in the trenches and at close quarters with the Russians which kindled the demand for some form of official recognition of the soldiers' gallantry.

The Distinguished Conduct Medal of the Crimean War: the first British gallantry medal, first awarded in 1855. Unusually, the obverse, shown here, does not bear the effigy of the Queen but the 'trophy of arms' design by Benedetto Pistrucci, which was also used on the Army Long Service and Good Conduct Medal.

As a result, three new awards were instituted during the war:

The Distinguished Conduct Medal, for 'Other Ranks' of the Army;

The Conspicuous Gallantry Medal, open to Other Ranks of the Royal Navy and Marines as a naval counterpart to the DCM;

The Victoria Cross, an award for conspicuous gallantry (or simply 'For Valour', as the medal itself states) which was open, most unusually for its day, to *all ranks* of the Army, Royal Navy and Marines.

For the Crimean War (including operations in the Baltic and Sea of Azoff), 111 VCs were awarded, about 670 DCMs and only 10 CGMs. Sixty-two of the first VCs were personally presented by Queen Victoria in a grand review in Hyde Park in 1858, their recipients being the centre of attention of the crowds of people and journalists. Many servicemen also received decorations from the French, Turkish and Sardinian allies, some of these being for acts of gallantry. The concept of bars (the clasps worn on the ribbon as indications of further awards) also appeared at this time, being instituted with the VC.

It has always been difficult to decide exactly who should earn which medal and for what actions: one act of gallantry that received, say, the DCM can seem just as brave as another for which the VC was awarded. It has also become increasingly hard to earn any decoration as there is no doubt that the degree of gallantry required has increased since the middle of the nineteenth century. Nevertheless, the principle of granting medals for bravery in the field was firmly established with the institution of these awards; it was to develop over the next hundred years into a fully fledged system of official gallantry awards.

Some general points

Institution
New awards normally emanate from the monarch and are instituted by Royal Warrant.

Verifications and citations
Notifications of all official awards for gallantry down to Mention in Dispatches level, including foreign decorations but not cards and certificates, are published in *The London Gazette* (or its colonial and dominion equivalents, like *The Gazette of India*) where the terms and conditions of the award are also laid down. *The London Gazette* has indices that list recipients alphabetically by award. In many instances, citations (that is, details of the action for which the award was made) are also published, though often in a later *Gazette*. In general, the earlier awards have less detail on the action: there are often only a couple of lines on early awards of the Victoria Cross, and most Victorian Distinguished Conduct Medals state little other than the theatre of war. A great deal of extra information can often be found in regimental histories or local newspapers, whilst Victorian periodicals like *The Illustrated London News* frequently carried stories of acts of gallantry or presentations of awards. During the First World War citations for all gallantry awards tended to be published in detail, except for the Military Medal (for which few citations survive) and foreign awards, although awards notified in the New Year's Honours and the King's Birthday Honours did not usually have published citations. In the Second World War citations were not generally published – again, regimental histories and registers of awards (see Further Reading, page 61) can often provide details, and many original documents such as recommendations for awards, rolls of recipients and citations for most 1939–45 decorations can be found in the Public Record Office, Kew.

Obverse
The side of the medal generally bearing the monarch's effigy and titles. As crosses are plain on the reverse the obverse of crosses carries the main design.

Reverse
The side of the medal bearing a design, which often has an allegorical or symbolic significance, or (as on many British gallantry medals) simple wording. The reverse of crosses is usually plain and may be privately engraved with the recipient's details.

The obverse of a medal usually carries the effigy and titles of the reigning monarch. This example shows the 'crowned head' obverse of George V used only between c.1930 and 1936. Gallantry medals with this obverse are very rare.

Sizes

Most circular medals are a standard 35 mm in diameter. Crosses vary but are usually in the range of 40–50 mm.

Suspension

The means of carrying the ribbon and attaching it to the medal disc or cross.

Naming

Most British awards are either issued officially named around the rim (in the case of medals) or have plain reverses that can be named by the recipient (in the case of most crosses). Those officially named are hand-engraved, in a variety of styles, or have the personal details impressed by machine.

Bars

These are plain or decorated metal bars worn on the ribbon to indicate a further award. There is no limit to the number of bars that can be worn, though no British gallantry award has had more than three bars, in other words four awards of the decoration. Bars normally slip over the ribbon and may also be stitched down. When ribbons alone are worn, the possession of a bar is commonly indicated by a silver rosette unless otherwise stated below. One rosette is worn for each bar awarded.

Left: *Further awards of the same decoration are indicated by bars worn on the ribbon. This Distinguished Conduct Medal of 1914–18 has a bar of the laurelled type used on a number of British gallantry awards. It simply slides over the ribbon and is not attached to the medal suspension.*

Above: *When ribbons alone are worn in uniform, the possession of a bar is generally shown by the wearing of a small silver rosette on the appropriate ribbon. This one is on the ribbon of the Military Cross, indicating two awards of that decoration.*

Ribbons

Most ribbons are standardised at 32 mm wide. In some instances (the George Cross and George Medal, for example) awards to women are worn suspended from a bow of medal ribbon.

Forfeiture

Decorations are officially conferred as honours and most carry terms of forfeiture – they could be taken away and the award cancelled in the case of serious misdemeanour or if the recipient received a criminal conviction, even at a much later date.

Posthumous awards

It is now usual for the next of kin of an award winner who was killed in action or died to receive the medal he or she would have been given. This has not always been the case: at first the Victoria Cross could not be awarded posthumously, *The London Gazette* simply announcing that it would have been conferred had the recipient survived. The practice changed during the reign of Edward VII. In many instances, where no terms allowed posthumous award, a Mention in Dispatches was the only honour that could be conferred, and until after the First World War there was no visible indication that an MID had been awarded.

Awards to foreigners

Many British gallantry awards can be conferred upon foreign nationals for services rendered with British forces; this was especially so during the two world wars. Such awards are not usually named and are not usually published in *The London Gazette*.

Post-nominal letters

Some award terms specify that the recipient may use letters after his name to indicate possession of the award; others were amended to do so (for example 'DCM' or 'MM' after 1918 for recipients of the Distinguished Conduct Medal and Military Medal). Some are not specific but by tradition recipients do use post-nominal letters (as with the Distinguished Service Order, for example).

Design and manufacture

The majority of medals were designed by the resident artists of the Royal Mint and most were also made there. Some medals were made elsewhere: the Distinguished Flying Cross and Air Force Cross, for instance, were produced until *c.*1921 by Pinches of London, the obverses being designed by the Liverpool sculptor and well-known medallist E. Carter Preston, and the VC has always been manufactured by Hancocks of London – the only medal or decoration they produce. The royal effigies used as the obverse of most medals are generally the work of Royal Mint artists, using officially approved designs, many of which also appear on contemporary coins and stamps as the standard image of the monarch. Medal ribbons are usually designed by the Royal Mint but their manufacture can be contracted out to companies such as Toye, Kenning, Spencer.

The Russian War, 1854–6: British warships in action in the Black Sea. The first Victoria Cross ever awarded went to the Royal Navy during this war, to Lieutenant Charles Lucas of HMS 'Hecla', for gallantry in the Baltic in 1854. The Conspicuous Gallantry Medal was also inaugurated, as a Royal Navy and Royal Marines' equivalent of the Distinguished Conduct Medal, though only ten were awarded.

The gallantry awards

The awards are listed here in their official 'order of precedence', in other words the order in which they are worn on the uniform in the case of multiple awards of decorations. Orders and gallantry medals are worn to the left of a medal group (as viewed), followed by campaign medals in date order, then jubilee and coronation awards, and lastly long service medals. Foreign awards are worn to the right of the group (as viewed) in their own order of precedence.

VICTORIA CROSS
Description: a cross pattée in bronze, chemically darkened, with the royal crest of a lion over a crown, above a scroll inscribed FOR VALOUR. Plain reverse, with a central roundel bearing the date(s) of the action(s) for which the award is made. Suspended from a ring and 'V' below a laurelled bar. A miniature VC is borne on the ribbon when ribbons alone are worn.
Instituted: Royal Warrant 29th January 1856; *London Gazette* 5th February 1856. First awards announced 24th February 1857.
Awarded to: initially open to all ranks of the Army, Navy and Royal Marines, and to Colonial forces; extended to the Indian Army in 1911.
Metal: bronze; by tradition, the metal is taken from Russian guns captured at Sebastopol, 1854–6.

Presented by the King: Sergeant Harold Whitfield of the 10th King's Shropshire Light Infantry receives the Victoria Cross from King George V in a ceremony in Leeds in 1918. It was usual for such high awards to be presented by the King. Sergeant Whitfield's VC is illustrated below and is now on display in Shrewsbury Castle.

Naming: engraved on the reverse of the suspension bar with number, rank, name and unit. Date of action(s) in central roundel.

Bars: authorised in the original Warrant. To date only three bars have been awarded. Since 1918 a miniature VC is worn on the ribbon to represent the bar when ribbons alone are worn.

Ribbon: originally dark red for the Army; dark blue for the Navy and Royal Marines. Standardised to dark red for all services in 1918.

Above left: *The Victoria Cross, obverse. Instituted in 1856, it remains the highest award for gallantry. It is made by Hancocks of London, each one hand-chased to sharpen the detail and chemically darkened. By tradition, Hancocks use bronze taken from Russian guns captured during the Siege of Sebastopol.*

Above right: *The Victoria Cross, reverse. The recipient's name and details are lightly engraved on the suspension bar and the date of the action or actions for which it is conferred is engraved in the centre. This example was awarded to Private (later Sergeant) Harold Whitfield, 10th King's Shropshire Light Infantry, for gallantry in Palestine in 1918, when he single-handedly attacked and captured a Turkish machine-gun position.*

15

Lord William Beresfor‹ in personal combat with a Zulu on the Umvolosi river on 3rd July 1879, during the Zulu War. He was awarded the Victoria Cross for this action, in which he rescued a wounded soldier who had fallen from his horse and carried him to safety. Twenty-three VCs were granted for this campaign, along with fifteen Distinguished Conduct Medals.

The VC is awarded for 'acts of conspicuous courage and bravery under circumstances of extreme danger'. It is the highest ranking British award for gallantry and only 1354 have been granted since 1856, all to men. It has been awarded to civilians and for services not 'under fire'. A monetary pension accompanies the award. Much has been written about the VC and its recipients, and some actions resulting in its award are justifiably famous, such as the eventual eleven awards for the Defence of Rorke's Drift in the Zulu War, 22nd–23rd January 1879.

Citation for the Victoria Cross awarded during the Boer War, 1899–1902, to Shoeing Smith Alfred E. Ind, Royal Horse Artillery.

On Dec. 20th 1901 near Tafelkop, Orange River Colony, South Africa, Shoeing Smith Ind stuck to his gun under very heavy fire when the whole of the remainder of the team had been shot down, and continued to fire into the advancing enemy until the last possible moment. A Captain who was mortally wounded on this occasion requested that Shoeing Smith Ind's gallant conduct on this and on every other occasion since he joined the service be brought to notice.

Winning the Victoria Cross: Sergeant George Eardley, 4th King's Shropshire Light Infantry, was awarded the VC for conspicuous gallantry in Holland in October 1944. He single-handedly attacked and destroyed a series of German machine-gun positions in orchards near Overloon. He had already been awarded the Military Medal for gallantry in Normandy. (Sketch by Bryan de Grineau, Shropshire Regimental Museum)

The Victoria Cross and Indian Mutiny Medal with three clasps awarded to Private Robert Newell, 9th Lancers, for gallantry in rescuing a comrade under heavy fire at Lucknow in March 1858. Newell did not live to wear the award: he died of disease at Ambala shortly afterwards.

Citation for the Victoria Cross awarded during the Second World War to Private J. Stokes, 2nd King's Shropshire Light Infantry, 1944.

On March 1st 1945, during an attack on Kervenheim, Rhineland, a platoon was pinned down by intense rifle and machine-gun fire from a farm building. Pte Stokes dashed into the building, firing from the hip, and appeared with 12 prisoners. During the operation he was wounded but refused to go to the regimental aid post and continued the advance with his platoon and rushed another house, taking 5 more prisoners. Now severely injured, he insisted on taking part in the advance on the final objective but fell mortally wounded 20 yards from the enemy position.

CONSPICUOUS GALLANTRY CROSS

Description: silver cross pattée, the arms joined by sprays of laurel. Central roundel with crown. Plain reverse, bearing recipient's details. Suspended by a ring from a plain silver bar.
Instituted: October 1993. First awarded in 1995 for service in Bosnia.
Awarded to: all ranks of the armed forces for gallantry in action.
Metal: silver.
Naming: details impressed on the reverse.
Bars: none issued to date.
Ribbon: white with blue edges and central red stripe.

As early as the 1930s there were calls for the system of awards to be reformed, especially to remove the distinction in gallantry awards between officers and Other Ranks and to simplify what had become a complex mixture of qualifications and honours. The issue proved controversial, with 'hard-liners' putting up a largely successful opposition to change. The reform calls were periodically revised, most recently by John Major, who when he was Prime Minister forced a complete review of military honours and inaugurated sweeping changes to the system in the 1990s.

In 1993 a new high-level award, the Conspicuous Gallantry Cross, was instituted and other gallantry awards became available to all ranks, with those previously granted only to Other Ranks being abolished. This meant the end of the Distinguished Conduct Medal along with the Military Medal, the Distinguished Service Medal, the Distinguished Flying Medal and the Air Force Medal, as well as the two Conspicuous Gallantry Medals. Their officer equivalents – the Distinguished Service Order, the Military Cross, the Distinguished Service Cross, the Distinguished Flying Cross and the Air Force Cross – thus became available to *all* ranks.

The first award of this high-ranking decoration was made to Corporal Wayne Mills of the Duke of Wellington's Regiment for gallantry in Bosnia in 1994.

The Conspicuous Gallantry Cross was created during the reforms of 1993 as a 'classless' decoration and was first awarded for service in Bosnia in 1995 in the aftermath of the Balkan civil wars. The reverse is plain except for the recipient's details.

The George Cross, obverse. Instituted in 1940, it is primarily regarded as a civilian decoration but many have been issued to military recipients for great gallantry whilst not under fire. The reverse is plain except for the recipient's details and date of publication in 'The London Gazette'.

GEORGE CROSS

Description: a plain silver Greek cross with a central medallion depicting St George and the dragon, around which are the words FOR GALLANTRY. In the angle of each arm of the cross is the royal cypher G.VI. Plain reverse, bearing recipient's name and date of award. Hangs from a straight laurelled bar attached to the cross by a small ring and lugs.

Instituted: Royal Warrant 24th September 1940; *London Gazette* 31st January 1941.

Awarded to: military and civilian recipients, male and female. The most unusual award is that to the island of Malta in 1942, honouring the population as a whole for their fortitude and gallantry in defence of the island.

Metal: silver.

Naming: engraved in upright capitals with name and (where appropriate) rank and branch of service, along with *London Gazette* date of notification – not the date of the deed for which the award is made.

Bars: authorised in the original Warrant but none so far awarded.

Ribbon: plain blue. Female recipients wear the medal from a bow fashioned from the medal ribbon. A miniature GC emblem is carried on the ribbon when ribbons alone are worn.

The GC is the highest *civilian* award for gallantry, granted only 'for acts of the greatest heroism or of the most conspicuous courage in circumstances of extreme danger'. Also awarded to police, fire and rescue services, it has been awarded to members of the armed forces, generally in actions other than under enemy fire (for example bomb disposal or saving lives on minefields) and in circumstances where purely military awards are not appropriate. Fewer than 150 have been granted, excluding exchanges of the Empire Gallantry Medal (see page 50). Since 1965 an annual pension (originally £100 per annum) has been paid to recipients. Recent awards have been posthumous.

Part of a George Cross group to the Royal Air Force, worn with Second World War stars and medals.

19

A Victorian Distinguished Service Order: Lieutenant-Colonel Norton Legge of the 20th Hussars served in Egypt and the Sudan, 1885–6, and again in the Sudan in 1896–8. He was awarded the Distinguished Service Order (seen here to the left of his medal group) in 1896 for 'recent operations in the Sudan'. He was killed in action during the Boer War.

DISTINGUISHED SERVICE ORDER

Description: a gold-edged cross, enamelled white with a green central wreath containing the Imperial Crown in gold on a red enamel background. The reverse has, in the centre of the cross, the cypher of the reigning monarch below a crown, within a green wreath on a red enamel background.

Instituted: Royal Warrant 6th September 1886; London Gazette 9th November 1886.

Awarded to: commissioned officers, Army, Navy and Colonial; in 1918 extended to the Royal Air Force and in 1943 to the Merchant Navy and Home Guard. In 1993 all ranks became eligible for the DSO 'for leadership'.

Metal: until 1889–90 gold and enamel (approximately 150 issued); thereafter silver gilt and enamel.

The reverse of the Distinguished Service Order showing the post-1901 crown. It was instituted in 1886 to reward junior officers for distinguished service, but many were awarded for specific acts of gallantry on campaign. Since 1993 it has been open to all ranks, but for qualities of leadership, not gallantry.

Above: *The obverse of the Distinguished Service Order, with the cypher of the reigning monarch, in this case King George V.*

Above: *Air support: a novel feature of the First World War was the use of aircraft to spot enemy guns and troop movements from above and report them back to British artillery positions. Here, Lieutenant Swan Lewis earns the Distinguished Service Order for carrying out low-level observation under ground fire.*

Varieties: variations in manufacturer mean that there are minor differences in the crowns. Some variation in thickness, with earlier awards tending to be much thinner.

Naming: unnamed. Occasionally seen with privately engraved details on the edges of the arms of the cross or the reverse of the suspension bar.

Bars: authorised 23rd August 1916; plain silver with small central crown. From 1938 engraved with year of award on reverse.

Ribbon: wide central stripe of red, flanked by narrower stripes of dark blue. The ribbon is slightly narrower than standard and hangs from a laurelled brooch bar.

Left: *The Distinguished Service Order with three clasps, one of only a handful of such multiple issues conferred, indicating no less than four separate awards of the DSO for 1914–18 and representing a truly outstanding record of service.*

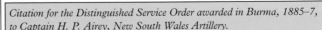

Citation for the Distinguished Service Order awarded in Burma, 1885–7, to Captain H. P. Airey, New South Wales Artillery.
For distinguished service, coolness under fire and marked gallantry.

A fine gallantry group: the Distinguished Service Order with second award bar and the Military Cross, along with campaign awards for 1914–18 and medals for 1939–45. The recipient was Major G. C. Richardson, Royal Horse Artillery.

British infantry going into action during the Boer War: men of the Royal Scots Fusiliers pursue the enemy during the guerrilla war phase of the fighting in 1901. Seventy-eight Victoria Crosses, approximately 1140 Distinguished Service Orders and just over 2000 Distinguished Conduct Medals were awarded for this long and difficult campaign in South Africa, 1899–1902.

An early gold Distinguished Service Order, awarded to Lieutenant S. F. Judge, Egyptian Army, for gallantry at Toski in the Sudan in 1889. Shown with his Egypt Medal (1882–8) with clasps Gemaizah 1888 and Toski 1889 and the medal for the Sudan, 1896–8.

The DSO was established as an 'Order' and recipients were 'Companions' appointed to the Order. It was intended as an award for junior officers and for services for which the Companionship of the Order of the Bath would not be appropriate. It could be conferred for specific acts of gallantry or more generally for distinguished service over a period, though initially recipients had to have been mentioned in dispatches. After 1917 it came to be granted for gallantry in action. It became obsolete as an award for gallantry in 1993 upon the introduction of the Conspicuous Gallantry Cross but has been retained as an award for leadership open to all ranks.

> *Citation for the Distinguished Service Order awarded during the First World War to Lieutenant (acting Lieutenant-Colonel) G. S. Brighten, Liverpool Regiment, 1918.*
>
> For conspicuous gallantry and devotion to duty during an enemy attack. He was commanding the battalion in reserve and employed it to such advantage that the attack was held up and the enemy repulsed with heavy loss, many prisoners being taken. His clever disposal of his forces and his coolness under fire did much to restore the situation.

The obverse of the Distinguished Service Cross. Like the Military Cross, this is a very simple but elegant silver cross; its obverse bears only the cypher of the monarch, the reverse being absolutely plain except for the year of award (after 1940) and any personal details the recipient might have had privately engraved.

DISTINGUISHED SERVICE CROSS

(originally the Conspicuous Service Cross, 1901)

Description: a plain silver cross with convex ends to the arms, the obverse bearing the reigning monarch's cypher in a central roundel. Plain reverse; after 1940 the year of award is engraved on the lower arm. Suspension by a silver ring.

Instituted: originally in June 1901 as the Conspicuous Service Cross. By Order in Council of 14th October 1914 designated the Distinguished Service Cross.

Awarded to: warrant officers and junior commissioned officers of the Royal Navy below the rank of Lieutenant Commander; extended in 1931 to Merchant and Fishing Fleets, in 1940 to Royal Air Force and in 1942 to Army personnel serving afloat. From 1993 available to all ranks.

Metal: silver.

Naming: issued unnamed but sometimes seen with details privately engraved.

HMS 'Gloucester' engages the German warship 'Breslau' off Cape Matapan on 7th August 1914. For gallantry in actions such as this, apart from the Victoria Cross and the Distinguished Service Order, naval officers could be rewarded with the Distinguished Service Cross and other ranks with the Conspicuous Gallantry Medal or Distinguished Service Medal. Submarine warfare added a new element to combat at this time and naval awards were also granted to the Merchant Navy.

Bars: authorised 7th September 1916. Plain slip-on type, with convex ends and central crown. Plain reverse until 1940, after which it bears the date of award. Only one issued with three bars.

Ribbon: three equal stripes of dark blue, white and dark blue.

The DSC was originally instituted in 1901 as the Conspicuous Service Cross for junior commissioned officers and warrant officers of the Royal Navy, for 'meritorious or distinguished services in action'. Only eight awards were made before 1910, so the Edward VII obverse is very rare. Since 1914 about 7500 crosses and bars have been awarded, with some 4500 of these for 1939–45. Following the reforms of 1993 it is now available to all ranks, the Distinguished Service Medal (for Other Ranks) being rendered obsolete.

> *Citation for the Distinguished Service Cross awarded to Commander Edward Smith, RN, HMS Argonaut, 1942.*
>
> For bravery and skill in HM ships *Aurora*, *Sirius*, *Argonaut*, *Quentin* and HMAS *Quiberon* in a brilliant and successful action against an escorted Italian convoy in the Mediterranean in which four ships of the enemy convoy and two enemy Destroyers were sunk.

25

The obverse of the Military Cross showing the cypher of George V, as awarded during the First World War to warrant officers and officers below the rank of Major.

MILITARY CROSS

Description: a plain Greek cross, with splayed ends to the arms, each of which bears the imperial crown. The obverse centre bears the monogram of the reigning monarch. The reverse is absolutely plain, unless the recipient had details privately engraved. Between *c.*1938 and 1957 the year of award was engraved on the reverse of the lower arm. Suspension via a plain, flat bar with a small ring.

Instituted: Royal Warrant 28th December 1914; *London Gazette* 1st January 1915. First awards published 1st January 1915.

Awarded to: originally warrant officers and junior commissioned officers of the Army, including Colonial and Indian forces. Could also be granted to Royal Marines' officers, and a few were given to Navy and Air Force officers. Since 1993 available to all ranks.

Metal: silver.

Left: *The obverse of the Military Cross with the 'GRI' cypher, awarded between 1937 and 1947 and reflecting George VI's status as Emperor of India. After Indian independence in 1947 the cypher was altered to a simple 'GviR'.*

The reverse of the Military Cross showing the dated lower arm, as issued between c.1938 and 1957. This is the year of publication in 'The London Gazette', which is not necessarily the year of the action for which the award was made.

A Military Cross group, showing the second award bar, both for 1918. The recipient went on to serve in the Second World War and wears 1939–45 campaign stars and medals in addition to his two medals for 1914–18.

Naming: issued unnamed but frequently found with details privately engraved on the reverse, often including date and place of action or 'Presented by the King'.

Bars: instituted 23rd August 1916. Plain, flat silver slide-on type, with central crown. After c.1938 the year of award is engraved on the reverse. Four recipients have received three bars.

Ribbon: white, with wide central stripe of purple.

A fine Military Cross group to a native Indian officer, awarded for Burma, 1945. In addition to two India General Service Medals (for campaigns on the North West Frontier, 1935 and 1936–7) and his 1939–45 awards, he has (far left) the Order of British India. Essentially a long-service award for Indian native officers, it could on occasion be granted for specific acts of gallantry or for distinguished service. At far right is the Indian 'overseas service' badge.

27

The Military Cross and Korean War medals awarded to Lieutenant A. G. Pack, King's Shropshire Light Infantry, for gallantry in Korea. His Cross bears the cypher of Elizabeth II.

The MC was designed as an award to warrant officers and junior commissioned officers of the Army 'for gallant and distinguished services in action', along the lines of the Distinguished Service Cross for the Navy. In January 1917 it was decreed that it should be awarded only for service *in action* and not, as had sometimes been the case, simply for generally meritorious war service. Approximately 40,000 crosses and bars were awarded for the First World War, 380 including bars between the wars (for example, on the North West Frontier of India) and about 11,500 for the Second World War. Since 1993 the MC has been available to all ranks.

Citation for the Military Cross awarded to Temporary Lieutenant J. B. Smeltzer, Machine Gun Corps, in 1918.

For conspicuous gallantry and devotion to duty. Although he was gassed before the enemy attack was launched, he remained in command and personally directed the fire of three guns. When one gun was put out of action he fired another himself until it was necessary to make good his withdrawal, which he effected successfully to a new position. By his cool and level-headed behaviour, he inspired all ranks with confidence.

A new type of warfare: air combat during the First World War was initially rewarded with army awards such as the Military Cross, Distinguished Conduct Medal and Military Medal for the Royal Flying Corps (later the Royal Air Force), or naval awards like the Distinguished Service Cross and Distinguished Service Medal to members of the Royal Naval Air Service. It was the distinctive form of air combat, however, which led in 1918 to the establishment of a series of new Air Force decorations: the Distinguished Flying Cross, Distinguished Flying Medal, Air Force Cross and Air Force Medal.

Below: *The obverse of the Distinguished Flying Cross. In contrast to the Military Cross and Distinguished Service Cross, the Air Force awards are highly ornate. This design is the work of E. Carter Preston.*

DISTINGUISHED FLYING CROSS

Description: an ornate cross flory, obverse with flaming bombs at the ends of three arms and a rose on the upper one. Superimposed on this is another cross formed of propellers, in the centre of which is a winged rose, below a crown with 'RAF'. Plain reverse with central roundel containing the reigning monarch's monogram and '1918', the date of institution.

Instituted: Royal Warrant and *London Gazette* 3rd June 1918.

Awarded to: originally to warrant officers and officers of the Royal Air Force; from 1993 available to all ranks of the RAF.

Metal: silver.

Naming: issued unnamed but sometimes found privately engraved on the reverse.

Bars: authorised in the original Warrant. Plain slip-on type, with RAF eagle device to centre. Since 1939 the date of award is engraved on the reverse.

Ribbon: originally intended to be alternating

29

A group containing the badge of a Member of the Order of the British Empire (MBE), military division (left), and the Distinguished Flying Cross with second award bar. There are also two medals for 1914–18 (with Mention in Dispatches emblem) and two for 1939–45.

horizontal stripes of violet and white, but changed in June 1919 to left–right diagonal stripes. It is not clear whether the horizontally striped version was ever issued.

Before 1918 personnel of the Royal Flying Corps (which became the RAF in April 1918) were awarded the appropriate Army gallantry awards, and the Naval awards in the case of the Royal Naval Air Service. The DFC was designed to recognise 'an act or acts of valour, courage or devotion to duty performed whilst on active operations against the enemy' under the very specific conditions experienced by air forces. It was the most extensively issued gallantry award for 1939-45, with nearly 22,000 including bars granted. Since 1993 the DFC has been available to all ranks; the Distinguished Flying Medal (for Other Ranks of the Air Force) was abolished.

Citation for the Distinguished Flying Cross awarded to Flying Officer Dennis David, RAF, May 1940.
Since dawn on 10th May 1940, this officer has shot down four enemy aircraft and shown gallantry and devotion to duty comparable with the highest traditions of the Service. His coolness and determination have been a fine example to the other Pilots of the Squadron. He was involved in an engagement when six other aircraft of the Squadron attacked over forty German aircraft in an attempt to protect Blenheim aircraft.

AIR FORCE CROSS

Description: an ornate silver cross in the form of thunderbolts, the arms joined by feathered wings, the lower arm ending with a bomb. Superimposed on this is another cross of propellers, the four ends inscribed 'G.V.R.I.'. Central roundel showing Hermes mounted on a flying hawk, proffering a wreath (see Air Force Medal obverse, page 49). Flat, plain reverse, except for a central roundel bearing the reigning monarch's cypher and '1918', the date of institution.

Instituted: Royal Warrant and *London Gazette* 3rd June 1918.

Awarded to: originally to warrant officers and commissioned officers of the Royal Air Force, the Fleet Air Arm, the Royal Navy and Colonial personnel. In 1993 the award was made available to all ranks of the RAF.

Metal: silver.

Naming: issued unnamed but sometimes found privately engraved with personal details on the reverse.

Bars: authorised in the original Warrant. Plain, silver slip-on type, with RAF eagle device to centre. After 1939 the date of award is engraved

Below left: *The ornate obverse of the Air Force Cross designed by E. Carter Preston, an established Liverpool sculptor.*

Below right: *The reverse of the Air Force Cross with simply the monogram of the reigning monarch and the date of institution of the award, 1918. This design is also used on the reverse of the Distinguished Flying Cross.*

31

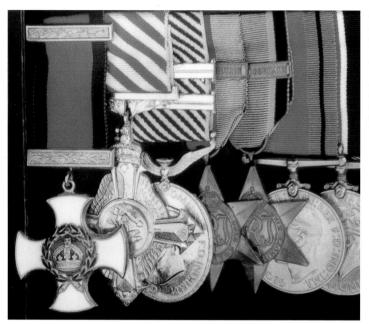

Part of a very fine group to a Royal Air Force officer who earned the Distinguished Service Order (left), the Air Force Cross and the Distinguished Flying Medal with two clasps: an outstanding range of awards.

on the reverse. Approximately twenty crosses have been awarded with two bars.

Ribbon: originally with alternating thin horizontal stripes of red and white. Altered in July 1919 to left–right diagonal stripes of those colours.

The non-combatant equivalent of the Distinguished Flying Cross, the AFC was granted 'for exceptional valour, courage or devotion to duty whilst flying, though not in active operations against the enemy' (for example test flights, transport, air–sea rescue), or for meritorious services. Citations are not usually published in *The London Gazette* for this scarce award, of which only about 5000 have ever been issued. Approximately 850 including fifteen bars were awarded between 1918 and 1939 and about 2000 during the Second World War. In 1993 the AFC was made available to all ranks of the RAF for non-operational gallantry (but no longer simply for meritorious service) and the Air Force Medal was rendered obsolete.

Citation for the Air Force Cross awarded to Wing Commander Dennis David, RAF, in January 1943. This officer has been employed on flying training since November 1941 and by his example, personality and ability has set a high standard and produced most creditable results. During this period of service there has been an increase in flying times and a marked decrease in accidents. Wing Commander David has been untiring in his efforts to improve the standards of training.

The Distinguished Conduct Medal: a Victorian issue, with 'trophy of arms' obverse. Shown here with the medal for the Ashantee War, 1873–4, clasp Coomassie, awarded to Sergeant William Little, Royal Engineers, for gallantry during the campaign in West Africa. Worn from an unofficial decorative brooch.

Below: The standard reverse of the Distinguished Conduct Medal used since its inception in 1854.

DISTINGUISHED CONDUCT MEDAL

Description: circular medal, the obverse originally bearing the 'trophy of arms' design by Benedetto Pistrucci used on the Army Long Service and Good Conduct Medal between 1830 and 1902. This was altered on the accession of Edward VII to show the reigning monarch's effigy and titles. The reverse has plain wording FOR / DISTINGUISHED / CONDUCT / IN THE FIELD. Ornate scroll suspension, swivelling until 1926, then fixed.

Instituted: Royal Warrant 4th December 1854. First awarded in 1855.

Awarded to: Other Ranks of the Army and Imperial forces but not to Indian soldiers.

Metal: silver.

Varieties: Colonial varieties exist, with 'Canada', 'Natal', 'King's African Rifles' or 'West African Frontier Force' added above the reverse wording. These are rare.

Naming: styles have varied over the years and frequently resemble those used on the relevant campaign medal. Post-1899 awards are usually impressed in plain block capitals of various sizes.

33

Action in Afghanistan, 1879: Gurkhas and British soldiers fight off an attack on their convoy at Korah. The two-year Afghan War led to the award of sixteen Victoria Crosses, 63 Distinguished Conduct Medals (including two bars) and 222 Indian Orders of Merit.

Below: *The George V obverse of the Distinguished Conduct Medal for 1914–18. For other ranks the medal was second only to the Victoria Cross as a reward for gallantry in action and was always greatly prized.*

Bars: authorised in 1881. Originally bore the date of the second action embossed in large capitals (for example 'MARCH 29th 1900'). From the beginning of 1917 this was altered to a straight silver laurelled bar.

Ribbon: crimson with a wide central blue stripe. A variant ribbon was worn on the King's African Rifles and West African Frontier Force versions (blue with narrow central light green stripe flanked on either side by a narrow stripe of maroon).

The DCM was effectively the first official British gallantry award, born out of the many acts of bravery in the field during the close fighting in the Crimea. Although Colonial

Citation for the Distinguished Conduct Medal awarded to Sapper E. Trask, Royal Engineers, during the Boer War, 1899–1902.
For coolness and gallant behaviour whilst building a sandbag wall across the railway bridge at Langerwachte Spruit, Feb. 23rd 1900, under heavy fire.

34

A corporal wins the Distinguished Conduct Medal in 1915: John Windell of the 2nd South Lancashire Regiment was sent to recover an abandoned machine gun. Seeing German troops massing below him, he opened fire on them and silenced their machine gun when it fired back. Eventually forced out of the house by German shelling, he later went back and brought out the gun.

A Victorian Distinguished Conduct Medal for South Africa in a group: two medals for the Boer War and three for the First World War. Far right is the Corps of Commissionaires long-service award. The recipient, Gunner Billingham, received the DCM for gallantry in trying to save the guns of 66th Battery, Royal Field Artillery, at the Battle of Colenso in December 1899.

Multiple gallantry: a group with Distinguished Conduct Medal, Military Medal and Mention in Dispatches for 1914–18 and a later award of the Meritorious Service Medal (far right). Also shown are three medals for the First World War, the 1939–45 Medal and the Army Long Service and Good Conduct Medal. Awarded to Sergeant W. C. Farringdon, Royal Artillery.

troops were eligible it was not granted to Indian soldiers, who had the Order of Merit and later the Indian Distinguished Service Medal. The DCM was awarded with a variable monetary gratuity and, after January 1918, recipients were permitted to use the letters 'DCM' after their name. The medal became obsolete in 1993 on the institution of the Conspicuous Gallantry Cross.

Citation for the Distinguished Conduct Medal awarded during the First World War to Sergeant F. C. Clark, 1st King's Shropshire Light Infantry.

On the 21st–22nd March 1918, at Lagnicourt, this NCO was holding a trench defending Battalion HQ and although subjected to intense shell and machine-gun fire, he directed his fire on the enemy, inflicting many casualties. When he had almost run short of ammunition, he went forward to an old dump and brought some back. It was not until almost surrounded that he was forced to withdraw, fighting a rearguard action. When all the officers had become casualties, he took charge. He repeatedly went into the open to bring back wounded men. He cheered his men and his personal disregard of danger inspired great confidence.

CONSPICUOUS GALLANTRY MEDAL

Description: circular medal with effigy and titles of reigning monarch on obverse. Plain wording FOR / CONSPICUOUS / GALLANTRY on the reverse, below a crown and within a wreath. Those for the Crimea had this wording (except FOR) engraved on the reverse. On all later issues it is embossed as usual. Most Victorian issues have suspension of the ornate scroll type, though some later ones are of the straight bar type that became standard after 1901.

Instituted: Order in Council 13th September 1855; re-instituted by Order in Council 7th July 1874 after the Ashantee War.

Awarded to: Other Ranks of the Royal Navy and Royal Marines.

Metal: silver.

Naming: there is considerable variation in style; can be engraved or (later) impressed in various sizes of capitals, and some bear the date and place of the action on the rim.

Bars: none granted to the 1855 type, although one man (D. Barry, AB) received two medals for separate actions in the Black Sea and Sea of Azoff. After 1874 a standard flat laurelled bar, of which only one has ever been awarded.

Ribbon: originally three equal stripes, of dark blue, white and dark blue. Altered in 1921 to a white ribbon with narrow dark blue edges.

The CGM was the naval counterpart of the Distinguished Conduct Medal, awarded to 'men who might at any time distinguish themselves by acts of conspicuous gallantry in action with the enemy'. Only ten were awarded under the 1855 order, and these were simply examples of the current Meritorious Service Medal (dated '1848' on obverse) with MERITORIOUS SERVICE erased and CONSPICUOUS GALLANTRY engraved in its place – a poor expedient. The medal lapsed until 1874 when it was re-instituted at the conclusion of the Ashantee War. Awarded with a variable annuity. A rare medal, only about 240 having been issued since 1874. The CGM became obsolete in 1993 on the institution of the Conspicuous Gallantry Cross.

The Conspicuous Gallantry Medal obverse. On issues of the CGM of Edward VII (shown here) and George V, the King is shown in Admiral's uniform, since the award is intended for the Royal Navy and Royal Marines.

CONSPICUOUS GALLANTRY MEDAL (FLYING)

Description: as for the Conspicuous Gallantry Medal.

Instituted: Royal Warrant 10th November 1942; *London Gazette* 15th January 1943.

Awarded to: Other Ranks of the Royal Air Force and associated air forces such as the Royal Air Force Volunteer Reserve, Royal Canadian Air Force, Royal Australian Air Force.

Metal: silver.

Naming: engraved in plain sans-serif capitals.

Bars: instituted in original Warrant but none awarded.

Ribbon: light blue edged with narrow dark blue stripes.

An extremely rare award, with only about a hundred issued. Intended to be the Air Forces' equivalent of the Army's Distinguished Conduct Medal or the Royal Navy's and Royal Marines' CGM. Awarded for 'conspicuous gallantry in action against the enemy'. It became obsolete in 1993 on the institution of the Conspicuous Gallantry Cross.

Right: *The Conspicuous Gallantry Medal (Flying) with George VI 'first type' obverse. The only difference between this and the standard CGM is the central ribbon colour, which is pale blue instead of white.*

The Conspicuous Gallantry Medal (Flying) with campaign stars of the Second World War.

GEORGE MEDAL

Description: circular silver medal, bearing on the obverse the effigy and titles of the reigning monarch. On the reverse a fine figure of St George slaying the dragon, with the words THE GEORGE MEDAL.
Instituted: Royal Warrant 24th September 1940; *London Gazette* 31st January 1941.
Awarded to: British, Commonwealth and foreign military personnel and civilians.
Metal: silver.
Naming: usually engraved in upright serif capitals in a variety of styles. Some Army awards are impressed. Names are sometimes given in full (rather than by initials).
Bars: authorised in the original Warrant. Flat slip-on type with laurel leaf design. No-one has received two bars.
Ribbon: red with five equidistant narrow blue stripes. Female recipients wear the medal from a bow fashioned from the medal ribbon.

Below left: *The reverse design of the George Medal showing a spirited version of the combat between St George and the dragon, which symbolises the ability to overcome great obstacles with courage.*

The GM is essentially an award for civilian gallantry ('acts of great bravery'), for which it ranks next below the George Cross. Awards have been made to military personnel in circumstances not under enemy fire such as bomb disposal or rescue attempts, or where purely military awards would not be appropriate. About two thousand medals and twenty-five bars have been awarded, about half to military recipients. The GM is also awarded to police, fire and rescue services.

Below right: *The Elizabeth II obverse of the George Medal. This is the 'second type' obverse, used from c.1959, in which the titles 'Britt. Omn.' ('all of the British possessions beyond the seas') have been removed, reflecting the decline in Britain's imperial position.*

INDIAN DISTINGUISHED SERVICE MEDAL

Description: circular silver medal with the reigning monarch's effigy and titles on obverse. Titles in Indian version ('Kaisar-i-Hind' = 'Emperor of India') until *c.*1933, when replaced by standard abbreviated Latin titles. Plain reverse with wording FOR / DISTINGUISHED / SERVICE within a wreath. Ornate scroll suspension, which swivelled until *c.*1943, then fixed.

Instituted: Royal Warrant 25th June 1907; *London Gazette* 28th June 1907.

Awarded to: all ranks of the native Indian Army, Indian State Forces, Militias and Levies; extended in 1917 to non-combatant 'followers' such as grooms and water-carriers, in 1929 to the Royal Indian Marine, and in 1940 to the Indian Air Force.

Metal: silver.

Varieties: a new crowned obverse of George V was instituted *c.*1933; these are rare.

Naming: engraved or impressed with number, rank, full name and regiment. A number of different styles of naming were used.

Bars: instituted by Royal Warrant 13th June 1917; *London Gazette* 6th July 1917. Silver slide-on laurelled bar.

Ribbon: dark blue with a wide central stripe of crimson. The medal is often worn from a laurelled pin-back brooch-bar.

Left: The Indian Distinguished Service Medal showing the 'first' obverse, with the crowned effigy of Edward VII and title 'Emperor of India', as instituted in 1907. The titles were altered to standard Latin versions c.1930.

The standard reverse of the Indian Distinguished Service Medal used on all issues 1907–47.

The Indian Distinguished Service Medal (George VI obverse) worn with the India General Service Medal, 1936–9, clasp North West Frontier 1936–37, which bears the single oakleaf Mentioned in Dispatches emblem.

From 1837 the only medal for gallantry available to Indian soldiers was the Indian Order of Merit (see page 8). The IDSM was instituted to reward actions which, though worthy of recognition, did not reach the standards required for the IOM. It is rather scarce, with fewer than six thousand including bars awarded. The IDSM became obsolete in 1947 when India became independent. Approximately 3200 were awarded for 1914–20 and about 1200 for 1939–47, with the rest mainly for frontier fighting and inter-war campaigns such as Iraq, 1919.

An Indian Distinguished Service Medal group for gallantry in North Africa, 1942. Note the decorated brooch-bar sometimes seen with the IDSM. The recipient also has the campaign stars and medals for the Second World War, the Army Long Service and Good Conduct Medal and (far right) the Indian Army Meritorious Service Medal.

41

The Distinguished Service Medal, the Other Ranks' gallantry award for naval operations. On the Edward VII and George V issue (shown here) the King is portrayed in Admiral's uniform.

DISTINGUISHED SERVICE MEDAL

Description: circular medal of standard dimensions, the obverse bearing the effigy and titles of the reigning monarch. The reverse has a crown over the simple wording FOR / DISTINGUISHED / SERVICE, the whole within a wreath. Plain, flat suspension, of the swivelling type until 1941, but then fixed.

Instituted: Order in Council 14th October 1914.

Awarded to: originally to Other Ranks of the Royal Navy, ashore or afloat. Extended in 1940 to men of the Royal Air Force serving with the Navy and in 1942 to Army personnel serving afloat (for example Royal Artillery gunners) and to men of the Merchant Navy.

Metal: silver.

Naming: for 1914–18, in engraved serif capitals, with number, initials, surname, rating and name of ship and sometimes with date and place of the operation (for example 'Atlantic Ocean 20 Aug. 1917'). Later issues in small sans-serif capitals.

Bars: authorised 27th June 1916. Those for 1914–18 generally have the date of the action upon the reverse. Only six awarded with two bars and only one with three.

Ribbon: dark blue with two central white stripes.

The DSM was awarded for instances of gallantry mainly in naval operations, to those 'as may at any time show themselves to the fore in

Above left: *The standard reverse of the Distinguished Service Medal.*

Above right: *The George VI 'first type' obverse of the Distinguished Service Medal, c.1937–47, with the King's title 'Indiae Imp.' ('Emperor of India').*

action and set an example of bravery and resource under fire' but who would not merit the award of the Conspicuous Gallantry Medal. It is a relatively scarce medal: about 4500 including bars were awarded for 1914–18 and 7200 including bars for 1939–45; fewer than 60 after 1945. Some were granted to Allied servicemen, such as French and Russian sailors. The DSM became obsolete in 1993 when the Distinguished Service Cross was made available to all ranks.

Citation for the Distinguished Service Medal awarded to Petty Officer E. W. Edwards, RN, HMS Indomitable, November 1942.

For bravery and dauntless resolution while serving in HM ships when an important convoy was fought through to Malta in the face of relentless attacks by day and night from enemy submarines, aircraft and surface forces.

The standard reverse of the Military Medal. Instituted in 1916 and born out of the close fighting conditions of the First World War for the countless acts of bravery which merited reward but which fell below the standard required for the Distinguished Conduct Medal. The first gallantry award granted to women.

MILITARY MEDAL

Description: circular silver medal. The obverse has the effigy and titles of the reigning monarch; the reverse has the simple wording FOR / BRAVERY / IN THE FIELD below a crown and royal cypher, all within a wreath. Ornate scroll suspension, which swivelled until *c*.1926, then fixed.

Instituted: Royal Warrant 25th March 1916; *London Gazette* 5th April 1916.

Awarded to: Other Ranks of the Army, Colonial Forces and (from 1944) to the Indian Army. Women were declared eligible in June 1916 and foreign nationals could also receive the award. Also granted to personnel of the Royal Navy and air forces on occasion.

Metal: silver.

Varieties: two obverses of George V; the second, a crowned head, was used only 1930–6 and is rare.

Naming: impressed in plain block capitals around the rim. Some 1939–45 Indian awards (especially for Burma) are engraved in a variety of styles.

Bars: authorised in the original Warrant. Laurelled type, which slides loosely over the ribbon.

Ribbon: dark blue with three white and two crimson stripes.

A close-up of the laurelled bar, worn here with the Military Medal but used with a number of other gallantry awards to indicate a second or further award.

Presented in the field: Field Marshal Montgomery pins the ribbon of the Military Medal to the tunic of Sergeant D. Murphy, King's Shropshire Light Infantry. In ceremonies 'in the field' such as this, it was common simply for the ribbon of the decoration to be presented, the actual award being presented at a later ceremony or even sent by post.

Below left: *George V obverse of the Military Medal awarded in large numbers during the First World War. The King is portrayed in Field Marshal's uniform.*

Below right: *George VI obverse of the Military Medal. The award was extended to the Indian Army in 1944 and many Indians received awards for Italy and Burma for actions which fell below the standard required for the Indian Distinguished Service Medal. The medal was in all cases very well earned.*

A Military Medal group for Korea, with Korean War medals and the Africa General Service Medal, clasp Kenya. Awarded to Corporal G. Newton, King's Shropshire Light Infantry, for gallantry on 9th July 1952 in withdrawing a patrol under heavy fire.

The MM was born out of the close-combat conditions of warfare during the First World War and the need to recognise the almost daily acts of gallantry ('individual or associated acts of bravery') which fell below the standard required for the Distinguished Conduct Medal. Over 120,000 including bars were granted for 1914–20 and about 15,500 for 1939–45. Only one has been awarded with three bars. It was the first gallantry award for women, the first being conferred for service in France in 1916 and during the Easter Rebellion in Dublin in 1916. The MM was rendered obsolete in 1993 when the Military Cross became available to all ranks.

Citation for the Military Medal awarded to Sergeant J. Foley, 1st Herefordshire Regiment, France, 1918.
During the consolidation of a captured trench near Beugneux, July 31st 1918, and under a fierce enemy bombardment, Sgt. Foley showed much energy and ability in quickly organising a scheme of defence. He stood on the trench parapet without any regard to danger, encouraging his men and inspiring them with absolute confidence – a feeling of high moral value at a critical moment.

DISTINGUISHED FLYING MEDAL

Description: an oval silver medal bearing the effigy and titles of the reigning monarch on the obverse. The reverse has a figure of Athena Nike seated on an aeroplane, with a hawk rising from her right arm above the words FOR COURAGE. The date '1918' was added in 1938. The whole reverse design is contained within a narrow laurel-wreath band. The unusual suspension takes the form of feathered wings attached to the medal by a bomb.

Instituted: Royal Warrant and *London Gazette* 3rd June 1918.

Awarded to: Other Ranks of the Royal Air Force and associated air forces.

Metal: silver.

Varieties: two versions of the George V obverse; the one with crowned head was issued 1930–6 and is rare (about twenty-two were issued).

Naming: all issued officially named. For the First World War, impressed in large serif capitals; those for the Second World War engraved rather crudely in plain capitals.

Bars: authorised in the original Warrant. Plain silver slip-on type, with RAF eagle device to centre. After 1939 the year of award is engraved on the reverse. Only one issued with two bars.

The reverse of the Distinguished Flying Medal with the post-1938 addition of the date of institution, 1918. It is unusual in being an oval medal with diagonal stripes on the ribbon.

Ribbon: originally with thin horizontal alternating stripes of violet and white. Altered in June 1919 to left–right diagonal stripes of those colours.

The DFM was the Other Ranks' equivalent of the Distinguished Flying Cross. It was awarded for gallantry in the air, 'for an act or acts of valour, courage or devotion to duty performed while flying in active operations against the enemy'. It could also be conferred upon Colonial and Dominion personnel. Approximately 6700 including 61 bars were awarded during the Second World War. The DFM became obsolete in 1993 when the Distinguished Flying Cross was made available to all ranks.

Citation for the Distinguished Flying Medal awarded to Flight Sergeant G. F. Beurling, RAF, 1942.
Sgt. Beurling has displayed great skill and courage in the face of the enemy. One day in July 1942 he engaged a number of enemy fighters which were escorting a formation of Junkers 88s and destroyed one fighter. Later during the same day he engaged ten enemy fighters and shot two of them down into the sea, bringing his total victories to eight.

On the North West Frontier of India, 1930. This, the most turbulent area of the British Empire, provided plenty of scope for the award of gallantry medals to all kinds of British and Indian soldiers throughout the period 1855–1947.

AIR FORCE MEDAL

Description: an oval silver medal bearing the effigy and titles of the reigning monarch on the obverse. The reverse has a figure of Hermes mounted on a flying hawk, proffering a wreath. The date '1918' was added in 1938. The reverse design is contained within a narrow laurel-wreath band. The unusual suspension takes the form of feathered wings attached to the medal by a bomb, as on the Distinguished Flying Medal.

Instituted: Royal Warrant and *London Gazette* 3rd June 1918.

Awarded to: Other Ranks of the Royal Air Force.

Metal: silver.

Varieties: two versions of the George V obverse; the one with a crowned head was issued only 1930–6 and is rare.

Naming: all issued officially named. For the First World War, impressed in large serif capitals; those for the Second World War engraved in plain capitals.

Bars: authorised in the original Warrant. Plain silver slip-on type, with RAF eagle device to centre. After 1939 the year of award is engraved on the reverse.

Ribbon: originally with thin horizontal alternating stripes of red and white. Altered in July 1919 to left–right diagonal stripes of those colours.

The AFM was the Other Ranks' equivalent of the Air Force Cross. It was awarded for gallantry not under combat conditions: 'for an act or acts of valour, courage or devotion to duty performed whilst flying though not in active operations against the enemy'. It was also granted to Colonial and Dominion personnel. This is a scarce award, with only about 304 including 5 bars awarded between 1918 and 1939 and fewer than 260 (with no bars issued) for the Second World War. The AFM was rendered obsolete in 1993 when the Air Force Cross was made available to all ranks.

Citation for the Air Force Medal awarded to Flight Sergeant V. A. Clouder, RAF, June 1942.

This NCO had been a Flying Instructor at this school since 13th November 1939. During this period he has carried out his duties conscientiously and efficiently despite the fact that he has always wanted to become an operational Pilot. During his period of service at the School, he has flown 884 instructional hours by day and 117 instructional hours by night.

The reverse of the Air Force Medal with its complicated design featuring Hermes, the messenger of the gods. The medal was awarded for gallantry in the air but not under combat conditions, such as air–sea rescue work.

BRITISH EMPIRE MEDAL FOR GALLANTRY

(also known as the Empire Gallantry Medal)

Description: circular silver medal; on the obverse the seated figure of Britannia, with FOR GALLANTRY in the exergue and FOR GOD AND THE EMPIRE, the motto of the Order of the British Empire, around the design. Reverse with the crowned cypher of the reigning monarch surrounded by four heraldic lions; in 1937 this was altered to include the words 'Instituted by King George V'. Unusual in not having the reigning monarch's effigy. Suspension by straight bar from a laurel-leaf spray.

Instituted: Royal Warrant 29th December 1922.

Awarded to: military personnel and civilians.

Metal: silver.

Naming: engraved in serif capitals.

Bars: authorised 30th June 1937, but none awarded.

Ribbon: originally plain purple, but with a narrow central crimson stripe for military recipients. Altered in 1937 to rose-pink edged

Above left: *The reverse of the British Empire Medal, post-1937 version, with 'Instituted by King George V' added to the design. This is the reverse type used on King George VI issues between c.1937 and 1947. Note the distinctive suspension incorporating laurel leaves. Both this medal and the one on the right have the 'military' ribbon with central stripe.*

Above right: *The post-1922 obverse of the British Empire Medal, unusual in not showing the effigy of the monarch. This example has 'Meritorious Service' in the exergue; those awarded for bravery have 'For Gallantry' in the same position. The 'For Gallantry' obverse was not awarded after 1940.*

The silver oakleaf emblem worn after 1957 on the ribbon of the British Empire Medal to indicate an award for bravery. The BEM ceased to be awarded for bravery after 1974 with the institution of the Queen's Gallantry Medal.

with pearl-grey, with a central stripe of pearl-grey added for military recipients.

Only 130 of these awards were made, about half to military recipients, mainly for gallantry other than under fire. Its history is complicated as there came to be a number of awards covering much the same thing. Upon the institution of the George Cross in 1940 the EGM became obsolete and recipients (apart from foreign recipients who had received honorary awards) were asked to exchange it for the GC. Some, however, preferred to keep the original award, and others kept the EGM *and* received an exchange GC. In addition to the BEM for gallantry there was a parallel award for meritorious service, many of which had been granted for bravery during the Second World War to the Merchant Navy and Civil Defence formations, for example. After 1940 some people were still awarded the BEM for gallantry when the act of bravery was not deemed worthy of a GC or George Medal, which were much higher awards. In order to show that their award was for gallantry, after 1957 recipients wore an emblem of two crossed oakleaves on the ribbon. A miniature version of this emblem was carried on the ribbon when ribbons alone were worn. The BEM for gallantry, with the emblem of oakleaves, became obsolete in 1974 when the Queen's Gallantry Medal was instituted.

Citation for the British Empire Medal for Gallantry awarded to Havildar Ahmed Yar, Indian Mountain Artillery, during the Quetta earthquake, 1935.

In Sandeman Rd., Quetta, Ahmed Yar for a period of 5 hours worked in a hole fifteen feet below a very unsafe wall, rescuing a man who was eventually found to be unharmed. During this period there were several shocks of great intensity and in any of these there was the grave risk of being buried. He was on continuous duty from the time of the earthquake until the battery returned to its lines on the evening of June 3rd 1935, setting the highest standard of leadership.

The Queen's Gallantry Medal, 1974. Intended largely as a reward for civilian bravery below the standard required for the George Medal, it has also been awarded to service personnel.

QUEEN'S GALLANTRY MEDAL

Description: circular silver medal bearing on the obverse the effigy and titles of the monarch. The reverse has THE / QUEEN'S / GALLANTRY / MEDAL beneath a large crown flanked by sprays of laurel. Ring suspension.

Instituted: 20th June 1974.

Awarded to: civilians and military personnel.

Metal: silver.

Naming: impressed, with name and military unit if applicable.

Bars: authorised when originally instituted.

Ribbon: dark blue with thin central stripe of red flanked by stripes of silver-grey.

Replacing the British Empire Medal as an award for gallantry and its emblem of oakleaves, the QGM was introduced in 1974 to reward 'exemplary acts of bravery', primarily by civilians though military personnel can receive the award for actions not under enemy fire in which purely military decorations are not appropriate. It is also awarded to police, fire and rescue services. Fewer than six hundred have so far been awarded.

Citation for the Queen's Gallantry Medal awarded to Lance Corporal C. E. Tait, Duke of Wellington's Regiment, Ulster, 1979.

In October 1979, as regimental Medical Assistant with 1st DWR, he was a member of a patrol which came under fire from terrorists. Despite being badly wounded, he immediately went to the assistance of the driver, who was very badly wounded. Dragging him out of the line of fire, he rendered prompt and effective first aid which undoubtedly saved his life. His courage and calmness were worthy of the highest praise.

The reverse of the Queen's Gallantry Medal: a traditional simple reverse design incorporating wording.

The standard reverse of the Meritorious Service Medal used since 1848. A long-established non-commissioned officers' award for very long service, it was conferred for gallantry between 1917 and 1928, mainly for acts of bravery during the First World War in incidents not under fire, such as putting out ammunition fires or saving lives during grenade accidents.

MERITORIOUS SERVICE MEDAL FOR GALLANTRY

Description: circular medal with the reigning monarch's effigy and titles on the obverse, and the reverse with simple wording FOR / MERITORIOUS / SERVICE beneath a crown, the whole within a wreath. Ornate, swivelling scroll suspension until 1927, when fixed.

Instituted: 1847 for long service; 23rd November 1916 for gallantry.

Awarded to: other ranks of British and Colonial (but not Indian) forces.

Metal: silver.

Naming: impressed around the rim in small capitals.

Bars: Royal Warrant 23rd November 1916. Silver laurelled type.

Ribbon: crimson with three narrow white stripes.

The MSM was a highly regarded award to non-commissioned officers for especially long service. In 1916 it was made available as an immediate award to all ranks (below commissioned officers) and all services for meritorious non-combatant service during the war. In November 1916 it was extended to include gallantry, with about 435 such awards, though not usually for bravery in action. There is no visible difference between this MSM and the standard non-gallantry type. The award of the MSM for Gallantry was ended in 1928 when it was replaced by the British Empire Medal for Gallantry. For a while the MSM and the EGM/BEM coexisted: the MSM tended to be awarded to military personnel and the EGM/BEM to civilians.

Citation for the Meritorious Service Medal for Gallantry awarded to Private F. W. G. Gollop (and others), 2nd Dorset Regiment, 1921.

For gallantry and devotion to duty during a fire at the arsenal at St Thomas' Mount, India, on the night of 18–19th June 1920. These soldiers were the first to undertake the removal of the bombs from the immediate vicinity of the flames, which they continued to do until ordered to rejoin the guard. The work was of a highly dangerous nature involving risks of explosion.

The First World War. The almost constant fighting along the Western Front, as well as in Gallipoli, East Africa, Mesopotamia and elsewhere, led to the establishment of new decorations: the Military Cross (1914) and Military Medal (1916) for the Army, and the Distinguished Service Medal (1914) for the Navy. Mentions in Dispatches also came to receive visible recognition in the form of certificates and emblems.

MENTION IN DISPATCHES

Description: for 1914–18 and up to 10th August 1920, a spray of oakleaves in bronze. For mentions after 10th August 1920, a single bronze oakleaf. Since 1993, a single silver oakleaf. In each case, it is pinned or sewn diagonally on to the appropriate campaign medal ribbon.

The bronze oakleaf spray used to indicate Mentions in Dispatches for the period 1914–20. For 1914–18 it is worn only on the ribbon of the Victory Medal, if awarded.

54

The single bronze oakleaf emblem used to indicate Mentions in Dispatches after August 1920. Only one emblem is worn, irrespective of the number of times a person has been mentioned during the same campaign. It is now made in silver.

Instituted: January 1920; amended 1943 (to apply retrospectively) to the single oakleaf type.

Awarded to: personnel of all services and ranks mentioned in dispatches.

Metal: bronze, 1920–93; silver from 1993.

The practice of listing in military or naval dispatches the names of those (especially officers) who had rendered distinguished, meritorious or gallant services dates back at least to the early nineteenth century. But there was no visible sign of this distinction until the conditions of the First World War forced a change. As so many men and women had been 'brought to notice' but had received no actual award, it was decided to establish a simple emblem as a visible sign of this honour. For the First World War the MID emblem was to be worn only on the ribbon of the Victory Medal (if awarded) and for the Second World War only on the ribbon of the 1939–45 War Medal – not on other campaign stars. Otherwise it is worn on the ribbon of the relevant campaign medal or, if no medal has been issued, on the jacket where a ribbon would have been worn. Only one emblem is worn, no matter how many times the recipient has been mentioned in a particular campaign. The MID emblem is still awarded.

The reduced-size oakleaf spray emblem worn on a ribbon bar to indicate the award of a Mention in Dispatches during the period 1914–20.

Other awards and emblems

The **King's** (or **Queen's**) **Commendation for Valuable Service in the Air** was introduced in 1942 to reward meritorious service or gallantry in the air which fell below the standard required for the Air Force Cross or Air Force Medal. When granted to service personnel it is represented by the single bronze oakleaf emblem as for the Mention in Dispatches, which may be worn *in addition to* a standard MID emblem where both have been awarded.

A purely civil award, the **King's** (or **Queen's**) **Commendation for Brave Conduct** was instituted in the Second World War originally as a small plastic badge, but this was soon replaced by a spray of silver oakleaves worn on a medal ribbon or on the jacket if no medal has been awarded.

Cards and certificates

Shortly before the institution of the Mention in Dispatches emblem at the end of the First World War it was decreed that persons mentioned would receive an official certificate bearing their personal details and the *London Gazette* date (not that of the action). In addition to this, in both world wars it became

Left: *A divisional gallantry card issued by the Commanding Officer of the 12th Division, commending the distinguished conduct of a soldier in the 5th Berkshire Regiment in 1918. Although plain, such cards showed the recipient that his bravery had been noticed.*

A brigade gallantry certificate, issued by the 36th Brigade, which records the date and place of the action: '8th/12th August 1918 during the operations near Morlancourt'. Badges of the constituent regiments are shown.

56

A very ornate gallantry certificate produced by the 38th (Welsh) Division in 1918. In addition to the usual personal details, this has a long citation detailing the action which has been brought to notice.

common for army, divisional or brigade commanders to issue gallantry cards, commendation certificates and the like. There was no standard practice: some units and commanders showed rather more zeal than others, and some did not issue any, but it was one way of indicating that an act of gallantry, whilst not perhaps meriting a medal, had been noticed and recorded.

Foreign awards

Members of British forces on active service alongside their allies have frequently been rewarded with allied decorations, sometimes receiving a foreign award for gallantry but no British recognition. During the Crimean War, for example, many officers and men received the French Legion of Honour, the Turkish Order of Mejidieh (both in various classes) or the Sardinian Al Valore Militare. These were announced in the usual way in *The London Gazette*. Recipients of British awards, especially officers, frequently received an allied decoration as well. Similarly, in the campaigns in Egypt and the Sudan between 1882 and 1898, Turkish decorations (especially the Orders of Mejidieh and Osmanieh) were awarded to British personnel, mainly

An officer's group of decorations, medals and miniatures. Lieutenant-Colonel R. Grove served in the Crimea (medal far right) and received the French Legion of Honour (second from left) and the Turkish Order of the Mejidieh (second from right). Interestingly, his bravery during the attack on the Redan at Sebastopol was not rewarded by the British government.

A First World War group which has the British Meritorious Service Medal and the French Croix de Guerre with silver star (two medals on far right). The group also contains the Second World War Defence Medal and 1937 Coronation Medal.

A group comprising the Distinguished Conduct Medal and First World War medals, with the Belgian Croix de Guerre. The Allied governments had an 'exchange of awards' agreement, by which a certain number of decorations were allocated to each other for distribution to deserving servicemen.

officers, in recognition of the part played by Anglo-Egyptian forces on behalf of the Sultan in his dominions. At least some of these would have been to reward gallantry in a particular action.

Not surprisingly, there are many foreign decorations associated with service in the First World War and, to a lesser extent, the Second World War. It is not unusual to see British medal groups of either war bearing the French Legion of Honour or Medaille Militaire, the French or Belgian Croix de Guerre, Belgian orders and a whole range of awards from allies such as the USA, China, Italy, Serbia and Russia. These awards were usually notified in *The London Gazette* though not with any citation details. Unless the original documents still survive (which is not very often) it can be difficult to establish exactly what the award

Title page from a 1920 'London Gazette' announcing awards for the Afghan War of 1919. Founded in 1665, the journal is the official paper of the government, publishing acts of state, promotions, official appointments and proclamations. Gallantry awards often appear (as here) in the 'Supplement' sections.

British forces in Bosnia, 1995. The reorganisation of military honours in 1993, which attempted to introduce a classless system of awards, was first implemented during UN operations in Bosnia. The first awards of the new Conspicuous Gallantry Cross were made in 1995 for this theatre and Other Ranks have since received both the Distinguished Service Order and the Military Cross for service in the former Yugoslavia.

was granted for, unless a regimental history or local newspaper gives some clue. Collectors tend to show some suspicion towards groups with foreign awards which are not gazetted or documented – though they could be perfectly genuine. In general, recipients of foreign decorations during the world wars were given unrestricted permission to accept and wear the awards in uniform.

Further reading

There is a growing literature on gallantry awards (especially the Victoria Cross), though many books are specific to one decoration or campaign. Awards to officers can be confirmed in the various *Army Lists* and their *War Services* supplements. For all British forces and ranks, the alphabetical indices of *The London Gazette* will locate officially gazetted medals, mentions and foreign decorations, and will give citations for certain awards.

Apart from the unit or campaign histories which may cover the relevant period, essential reading is P. E. Abbott and J. M. A. Tamplin, *British Gallantry Awards* (Seaby, 1971), an excellent and thorough survey; Sir A. Wilson and Captain J. H. F. McEwen, *Gallantry* (OUP, 1939), is equally useful and full of interesting details on all types of British gallantry awards, military and civil.

Books which have listings to confirm or outline awards include:

The Register of the George Cross. 1990.
Abbott, P.E. *Recipients of the DCM 1855–1909.* J.B. Hayward, 1975.
Bate, C.K., and Smith, M.G. *For Bravery in the Field: the MM 1919–91.* Bayonet Publications, 1991.
Bowyer, Chaz. *For Valour: the Air VCs.* Airlife, 1992.
Brown, G.A. *For Distinguished Conduct in the Field: the DCM 1939–1992.* Western Canadian Distributors, 1993.
Buxton, D. *Honour to the Airborne 1939–81* (two volumes). Elmdon, 1993.
Carroll, F.G. *The Register of the Victoria Cross.* This England, 1988.
Clarke, J.D. *Gallantry Medals and Awards.* Patrick Stephens, 1993.
Creagh, Sir O.M., and Humphris, E.M. *The Distinguished Service Order, 1886–1923.* Reprinted by J.B. Hayward, 1978.
Creagh, Sir O.M., and Humphris, E.M. *The Victoria Cross, 1856–1920.* Reprinted by J.B. Hayward, 1978.
Duckers, P. *Reward of Valor: the Indian Order of Merit, 1914–18.* Jade Books, 1999.
Fevyer, W.H. *The DSC 1901–38.* London Stamp Exchange, 1991.
Fevyer, W.H. *The DSM 1914–1920.* J.B. Hayward, 1982.
Fevyer, W.H. *The DSM 1939–1946.* J.B. Hayward, 1981.
Fevyer, W.H. *The George Medal.* Spink, 1980.
McInnes, I. *The Meritorious Service Medal: Immediate Awards 1916–28.* Naval & Military Press, 1992.
Pillinger, D., and Staunton, A. *Victoria Cross Presentations and Locations.* Highland Press, 1981; reprinted 2000.
Sainsbury, Major J.D. *For Gallantry in the Performance of Military Duty* (the MSM for Gallantry, 1916–28). Samson, 1980.
Walker, R.W. *Recipients of the DCM 1914–20.* Midland Medals, 1981.
Wilson, A., and McEwen, J.H.F. *Gallantry.* OUP, 1939.

Such books are available from specialist dealers such as the Naval & Military Press, Unit 10, Uckfield Industrial Park, East Sussex TN22 5QE; telephone: 01825 749494; and Spink's, 69 Southampton Row, London WC1B 4ET; telephone: 020 7563 4000. Internet sites such as www.abebooks.com and www.bookmarque.com are useful for locating out-of-print works.

Places to visit and contacts

Comprehensive collections and displays of medals and decorations can be seen in many major national museums.

Imperial War Museum, Lambeth Road, London SE1 6HZ. Telephone: 020 7416 5320. Website: www.iwm.org.uk

National Army Museum, Royal Hospital Road, Chelsea, London SW3 4HT. Telephone: 020 7730 0717. Website: www.national-army-museum.ac.uk

National Maritime Museum, Greenwich, London SE10 9NF. Telephone: 020 8858 4422. Website: www.nmm.ac.uk

Royal Air Force Museum, Grahame Park Way, Hendon, London NW9 5LL. Telephone: 020 8205 2266. Website: www.rafmuseum.org.uk

Royal Marines Museum, Southsea, Portsmouth, Hampshire PO4 9PX. Telephone: 023 9281 9385. Website: www.royalmarinesmuseum.co.uk

Royal Naval Museum, HM Naval Base, Portsmouth, Hampshire PO1 3NH. Telephone: 023 9272 7562. Website: www.royalnavalmuseum.org

There are also over 150 local military and regimental museums around Britain, many with fine collections of orders, medals and decorations. The reader is advised to consult the current edition of *A Guide to Military Museums* by T. and S. Wise (Imperial Press, 2000) for details such as opening times.

Leading societies catering for collectors of medals and decorations include the Orders and Medals Research Society (Membership Secretary: PO Box 248, Snettisham, King's Lynn, Norfolk PE31 7TA) and the Indian Military Historical Society (Secretary: 33 High Street, Tilbrook, Huntingdon, Cambridgeshire PE28 0JP).

The original service papers, medal rolls, award recommendations, many citations, war diaries and other surviving documents are held in the Public Record Office, Ruskin Avenue, Kew, Richmond, Surrey TW9 4DU; telephone: 020 8392 5202; website: pro.gov.uk.

A number of internet sites now cater for medal collectors and researchers: the official Orders and Medals Research Society site (www.omrs.org.uk) is a good starting point, as is MedalNet (www.medal.net) for listings of medal dealers and military booksellers.

Major General P. Holland-Pryor leaves Buckingham Palace with his guests after receiving the Companionship of the Order of the Bath, the Order of St Michael and St George and the Distinguished Service Order for service during the First World War. All three awards were presented at one ceremony by King George V. There were many personal presentations by the monarch during the Great War, at Buckingham Palace, elsewhere in Britain and 'in the field'. It was, of course, not possible for all recipients to be given their award by the King in person.

Index